Jeremy Jones, Clumsy Guy

Written by Charnan Simon • Illustrated by Cary Pillo

Published in the United States of America by The Child's World®
PO Box 326 • Chanhassen, MN 55317-0326
800-599-READ • www.childsworld.com

Reading Adviser

Cecilia Minden-Cupp, PhD, Former Language and Literacy Program Director,
Harvard Graduate School of Education, Cambridge, Massachusetts

Acknowledgments

The Child's World®: Mary Berendes, Publishing Director

Editorial Directions, Inc.: E. Russell Primm, Editorial Director and Project Manager; Katie Marsico,
Associate Editor; Judith Shiffer, Assistant Editor; Caroline Wood, Editorial Assistant

The Design Lab: Kathleen Petelinsek, Design and Art Production

Library of Congress Cataloging-in-Publication Data

Simon, Charnan.
  Jeremy Jones, clumsy guy / written by Charnan Simon ; illustrated by Cary Pillo.
    p. cm. — (Magic door to learning)
  Summary: Jeremy discovers that when he takes his time and is careful, he is no longer clumsy.
  ISBN 1-59296-619-5 (library bound : alk. paper)
  [1. Clumsiness—Fiction.] I. Pillo, Cary, ill. II. Title. III. Series.
  PZ7.S6035Jer 2006
  [E]—dc22   2006001405

A book is a door, a magic door.
It can take you places
you have never been before.
Ready? Set?
Turn the page.
Open the door.
Now it is time to explore.

2 FOR
$1.00

Jeremy Jones was a clumsy guy.

"Oops!" he said when he
knocked over his glass of milk.

"I'm sorry!"
he said when
he bumped
into Grandma.

"Excuse me!" he said when he tripped over his sister's blocks.

"Jeremy Jones!" said his
mother. "Please watch
where you're going!
Slow down and be
more careful!"

13

"Okay!" said Jeremy. Then he
raced out the back door and
ran smack-dab into Dad.

One day, Jeremy was playing in his backyard. He almost stepped on a bird's nest that had fallen from the crab apple tree.

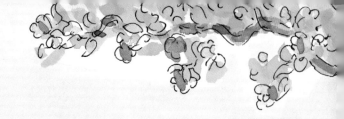

Jeremy started to grab the little nest.
Then he stopped to think. "Slow down,"
he told himself. "Be careful!"

Very, very carefully,
Jeremy picked up
the nest. Very, very
carefully, he lifted it
high and set it in a
fork in the tree.

Very, very happily, Jeremy watched
the mother bird fly back to her nest.

Jeremy Jones was not
always a clumsy guy!

Our story is over, but there is still much to explore beyond the magic door!

Do you know how much work goes into making a bird's nest? Try it yourself! With an adult's help, use mud, straw, grass, twigs, sticks, and string to build the best nest you can. Place hard-boiled eggs inside the nest to test its strength.

These books will help you explore at the library and at home:
Carle, Eric. *The Very Clumsy Click Beetle.* New York: Philomel Books, 1999.
Galloway, Ruth. *Clumsy Crab.* Wilton, Conn.: Tiger Tales, 2005.

About the Author

Charnan Simon lives in Madison, Wisconsin, where she can usually be found sitting at her desk and writing books, unless she is sitting at her desk and looking out the window. Charnan has one husband, two daughters, and two very helpful cats.

About the Illustrator

Cary Pillo lives in Seattle, Washington, and has been illustrating children's materials for twenty years. Besides drawing and painting, Cary enjoys swimming, bicycling, and baking (especially banana bread). She also spends way too much time playing with her little dog, Atlas, a trouble-making fox terrier.